T0166570

Hypotheticals
Leigh Kotsilidis

Coach House Books | Toronto

  Canada

Published with the generous assistance of the Canada Council for
the Arts and the Ontario Arts Council. Coach House Books also
acknowledges the support of the Government of Canada through
the Canada Book Fund and the Government of Ontario through the
Ontario Book Publishing Tax Credit.

LIBRARY AND ARCHIVES CANADA
CATALOGUING IN PUBLICATION

Kotsilidis, Leigh, 1976-
    Hypotheticals / Leigh Kotsilidis.

Poems.
ISBN 978-1-55245-249-3

    I. Title.

PS8621.O88H96 2011   C811'.6   C2011-904945-7

'In the beginning there was nothing, which exploded.'
— Terry Pratchett

Contents

III Falsifications

IV Conclusions

I
Evidence

Origins

Here is the whimper, the wrecked,
the weaker still. The underpinnings,
the crossbeams, the wilt. There is the bloodline,
fuse, the crux and heft. The basement,
blunt dark, the quantifiably bereft.
Where is the wattage of loss, decibel
of break, the blathering drain?
The receding spiral, formidable
slough, the ooze?

*

Here is lightning, meteorite,
flint. There, the amoeba, frog,
the feat. The eye socket, soft tissue
and ache. The spine, the cauliflower,
the bulb. The unpronounceable, synapse,
limbic drag and fall. Where is the mess hall,
the hearth, the mash? The egg, the ego,
the hut? Where is the matter? Here. Here
is the gust and here is the wreck. And here,
the inaudible bang.

By Any Name

When jackals' baying is both backdrop
and foreground, when forest

is conifers and impenetrable
fence, when mongoose predator

equals mongoose prey, which truth
will the brain feign?

A lyrebird's call appropriates
any sound it fancies. Above us,

shithawks flock
to mock us. Featherbrained,

we agree bullshit is the best
decoy. The average vocabulary

is 10,000 words, and one
easily stands in for another.

It is all the same.
For example, you, me

and the Cecropia moth,
born speechless, wriggling

free, only to flop atop
the first moth we see.

The Wayworn

We crash our balloon,
survive by a hare's breath,
which by morning
frosts.

We scrape it from trees
into the basins of our hands,
hold bark to the roofs
of our failing mouths.

The basket too small
to be a house.

Instead, we stress branches
to breaking points,
mingle treetops to a mess
dense as antler bone.

Suspend tatters
of balloon canvas
as signal, bellow them
like lungs.

For heat, we keep
our tempers stoked,
burn the thinning nests
of our hair.

Each day, we keep our ears
grounded for the pound
of the search party's hooves,
parting forest.

Inside this season so long
we've lost all need to name it.

Darwin's Family Tree

Take this fossil. Put your ear here.
Do you hear the electric hum,

the sum of related parts pooling
from epochs past? Now show me

the point where mouse
turns vole, where the distinctions

are not arbitrary. How to classify –
when new species pop up like finch,

when there is no stasis,
when every platypus, squid

and moose turns
to mulch. There must be a point

where the shadow of the moon stalls
long enough for two bodies to rise,

discreetly fall. Do you hear
what the tea leaves say?

My wind-stricken pine needs to know
which direction to throw its cones.

Sweet Tooths

The bees blast out of the nest,
blessed whizzing hearts a mess,
sticky legs fumbling for flowers
or familiar planters for platforms.

What matter threw them clear of home,
their midsections retrofitted to roam,
sailing over yacht-spattered ocean foam,
dive-bombing each spruced-up anaphylactic's

chrome-dome? If von Frisch were alive
he'd record the distance of sun from hive,
the relative shift of abdomen and wing,
nectar, stamen, sting. That there was no king

or that boredom could take hold, lost
in folds of paper scrap and serviette. No,
no naturalist or drone would believe
the queen sold off her succulent

golden throne for autonomy, despite
the heavy-duty dragooning, top-of-the-line
schmoozing. No. No way is *their* queen
on a beach, sucking cane-sugar cocktails,

high-fiving every dressed-to-impress CEO
who waggles for a wee taste of her comb.

Flypaper

Mobile
of mangled wings,
relinquished legs –

Eyelashes you saved
from her pillow
in an hourglass ampoule –

Yellow dress she left,
one with violets,
autopsied on the line –

Solubles

Rumours burn that lakes
will boil to their bottoms,
algae and plankton crackling
under a whip-wielding sun.

We know better than to believe
the buzz. Put our faith in hypotheses
so convincing even while sinking,
you mouth: *Gravity*.

There is a theory:
after a solid dissolves,
water recalls it as an oscillation
in the same range as the human voice –

I harvest lakes,
certain I will recover
where it is you sounded.

Lodged

A persistent westerly wrestles
the cotton of Kelvin's pillow, irks
the hammer handle in his ear,
yanks the strands that hook
his hippocampus.

On his forehead, anger barely bulges.
Instead, it grows five hundred metres
into his brain, one hundred kilometres
wide, festers against the insides
of his lobes.

Kelvin is about to explode
when she lets up,
one colossal wave
sloshes through the caverns
of his cranium –

The tools she's used to pick
his brain, every penny she's paid
for his thoughts, she watches
wash away. She doesn't linger
long enough to learn:

A kilometre up the slope
of his skull, whales skid ashore,
ships split, sleepy towns
slip to the floors
of fissures.

The Proof Is in the Pudding I

Like we are sessile
we stick to one spot

Watch how seagulls
salt the sea's field

We are not birds
with several angles of approach

How waves
jostle the light

It takes just one holler
to stall water's bonding

How the spaces inside our skulls
are never lulled

Along the length of every crack
lava solidifies

There is a slow collapse
on the horizon

At the heart of all matter
is a single, immutable point

Listen, climb in, I'll show you
what I mean by *rock*

what are we driving ourselves into

night is a candy
caught in our throats

fields tempt us
like mattresses

wires swing
like hammocks

dawn spills its guts
over the road

we swerve
to miss the mess

the truck tucks
itself up to the neck

in wheat
we could almost sleep

if it weren't for the vultures
at our throats

squabbling over
the last lozenge

of night
and the sunlight

boring in

Backhoe

An arthritic nimrod
roars orange,

angles an eye along an arm,
advances a fist.

Seams give way
under the skip-scrape.

You think of her dress –
your hand in the hem,

the underpass heaving
long strands,

asphalt slipping
from the shoulder.

Afterwards,
hush.

Diagnoses

You say the road ahead
is marrow.

On the horizon
birds fall apart. Clouds,

clusters of brain –
nebulous, cumulonimbus.

I say, let it rain.
Let it.

You say, but what comes after?

*

I say, somewhere at the edge of all this
a creek catches. Night

scrapes by on its poles. Swans
launch into flocks of bicycles. Wolves

bang at the moon. Insects' shells
crumble –

You say, it's the end.

I say, one of us is not normal.

Homo sapiens sapiens

We are not insects with exoskeletons,
nor is what's flesh and vulnerable about us

shielded by a supernatural force.
In most ways, we are more mackerel

than beetle, more grackles with spines
meant to bolster us from the inside.

Our softness stacking against us,
we are anxious –

At what point will we emerge from our centres?
Crawl from our corporeal dupes?

Watch: how mounds of land
smoulder from the mantle,

fields unsheaf, trees surge to fists,
puddles disperse into small grenades.

Who else, to say what is,
what will become of us.

Making a Comeback

A storm ripped
an expanse of artery.

Debris shifted to the back-
side of epidermis.

Vampire bats at the backlash
of a good walloping.

Wineglasses clanked
to the bash of an eye.

Who drives the limit
of bend-before-break?

The length of muscle
mongering after aftermath?

There is only the long overdue
and longing.

To not come back. Not make do.
Finally lose the wild goose.

Around every end
there is chase. A turn of evens.

Odd that we meet at all
without the culmination of lightning,

collision of skulls, or moons
crumbling. How can we know

whether raindrops will be wolves,
whether maplecopters swarm

or smother, when buoys go steady?
How can the wanton distinguish

come-on from warning?

Basic Instinct

Beached, your body curls deeper
into the conch, into the static
no-tones of sea foam. In here,
ears are wind-jammed to the piths,
there is no pitch to be had. You wish

this bold and steady wind to persist,
burst any encroaching nodule
of sound, so you won't be found.
For this cacophony to stave off
the most articulate groan

from your esophagus, sluice
through the most unequivocal
whistle a nostril can concoct.
Your body the antithesis of one-man
bands, fixed to stasis, without

the slightest derision of pulse.
No sudden betrayal, no beats
breaking in – that abominable
organ its straining strut.
You hope for nothing

of composure, the conversation,
as it stands, does not have
the constitution of an elephant.
Instead, takes the back seat, crosses
then uncrosses its legs.

II
Variables

Flight School

Which scientifically feasible theory alleviates
this, that or the other pang, the hang

and hunker of this or that man, the folly
of falling repeatedly off the lone horse,

the Morse of you, then you, then you and me?
That you or I are lonely or that this is only fling

would be no consolation to those known
as wingmen, the dartboard-hearted,

the dashed-hope guarded. That you or I
want more than less is not earth-shattering,

nor will it guarantee you or me the bee's
knees. No, one of us always buckles

and bucks beneath the spousal 'we,' needs
the other to believe there is no theory,

wants more then less, and more often
that and then another.

Sound Check

> *When the sentence, 'The spirit is willing, but the flesh is*
> *weak' was translated into Russian and then back to English,*
> *the result was 'The vodka is good, but the meat is rotten.'*
>   –John Hutchins

Have her undress, gown.
Now search for signs
of finger clubbing, cyanosis,
air hunger. While you visualize her
underlying anatomy's symmetry,
confirm her trachea
is midline. Put thumbs together
at her spine: *Breathe.*

To isolate districts of tenderness,
palpate her ribs, sternum.
Again: *Breathe.*
Is there turbulence
in the air flow? Is what you hear
dull? If it sounds at all like rubbing
hair between your fingers,
feathers on a snare,

have her whisper two
two-target tongue positions:
Toy boat. Blue balloons.
Toy balloons. Blue boat.
Don't let her fool you with coy
notes, lewd bassoons, buoyant
plumes, booze, croak.

Chest Wounds

First there is a flutter.
Not wings or eyelashes,
but a flap of unhinged skin.

What gapes? What gasps?
Not wound, windpipe or gash,
but lesions of men on a gauzy path.

Blades clank, clash, until shafts
sink in – a slowing, a lag, a yawn
as brains spawn panic.

Men stop, drop in their spots,
roll shirts into cotton batting,
tighten ponytails into tourniquets,

contort their torsos and limbs
into rocks resembling the dead.
When certain their enemy has fled,

toss their losses to the wind.
Not as seeds, words or hymns,
but overripe cherries, split to pits.

Punched In

It could have been struck
or starved. All we saw
was what we balked at:

a dead horse, not just at the doorstep
but already punched in,
vultures scrunched in every orifice,

all of them pecking through the day,
counting the seconds,
thirds, fourths and fifths,

only to pack it in at six –
to scrape the sky,
secure their nests, satisfy
those bottomless eggs.

Law of Averages

No dandy about town, no peerless
social lion.

Like everyone: down the hole of his ear,
around the corner, at the centre

is balance, the inner
earth 4,000 miles below.

Central Plaza is a stone's throw,
he works at Grand Central,

yet he stands outside the effects
of centring. Systems more comparable

to thought than gravity
guide his orientation. He cogitates:

What if a bird's wings malfunctioned?
Would its heart flop or flap?

What makes a sound structure snap
or dismantle?

If the world were flat
would his distance be understood?

He knows most things
are truly seen only from treetops.

That above all, there is no point
to reference, no centre of command.

That shortcuts,
like his shortcomings,

cause corrosion
and psychological damage.

There are no sunsets
at these serious latitudes.

When it's all up in the air
inevitably it drops –

Between here,
and here:

unpalatable coniferous,
untouchable terrain.

Fortune Teller

Churning out predictions,
our Gypsy Fortune machine warns
of whiteouts, snow squalls.

At the bottom of our mugs
sugar banks build at full crawl.

The next hours we navigate
like ploughs, cautiously turning,
careful to avoid.

You boil and bottle water,
seal off windows and doors,
I rummage through sideboard drawers
for something to warm my hands.

Later, when it seems the storm
has waned, we gather our nickels, wait
for the prickle, her carnival jaw jabbering:
molecular instability, nuclear failure.

The possibility?
Positively. Anytime.

In Equinox

The idea was change, or
at least rearrange our lives
to fit inevitable weather –

We bought fruit
camouflaged by bruise,
froze stews, thought we could make do
with what was left of preserves.

The idea was clemency, prepare,
avoid our tendencies
to move too quickly, to pick pears
that could stand to soften.

We stashed all we could
of birch sleeves, bagged leaves,
figuring we could always burn
our britches, our ancestral tweeds.

The idea was make it new,
at least attempt to make it through
a season we both knew better
than to bear.

Aerial View

She ladles lentil forests, carves
cliffs of meaty buffalo, plates
landscape after landscape. In the next
room her husband's appetite escalates
to the peak of the house.

At the open window
she contemplates the esophagus
of weather – how wind
shapes wood, how trees
always seem to lean away.

At the end of his rope,
her husband hauls the glider,
stacks bones at his feet. Between
them an unseen gap for her
to stash the wind.

parlour tricks

his passion defies the limits,
pins china and chairs against the fine weave of wallpaper,
flattens the scene into a figurine stuffing her own needs
with crumpets and tea, until her gown blooms like a balloon,
so taut threads begin to pop, one by one she becomes
a bombshell breaking an army

on the opposing slope, a soldier shines his boots
into puddles deep enough to swallow a limp, packs his rifle
with powder, the flour his wife uses to bake bread,
each morning rises with gunfire, hammers him hollow,
at the butt of a barrel, his only enemy the man who has come
to fill the gap

like the slow simmer of tapped sap,
some will pressure the pot, while others are content shelved,
constrained, she could have fit the entire cast of herself
in a satchel, small enough, she would have been stashed
about his neck, her weight pounding at his chest, distance
breached in each small explosion

Symbions

At the top of the hill, our mouths
hang open like airports.

Snow trajectories
slip in and out of view.

It is the fixed lines of palms
we navigate by.

When two points collide,
tumble symbiotically

through time, it is called
interstellar crystalline fusion.

Yet, how can we calculate rates
of expansion, identify thresholds?

How can we know when a union
has become parasitic?

Has it gone too far when flakes
the size of fists are hurtling toward our heads?

Almanac

Some stories are the same every time you hear them –
but you are not.
    – Ann-Marie MacDonald

This one begins with one of those
(if you were to blink) hit-or-miss
towns, where livestock outnumber
people five to one. Fields are unsown
corduroy. Seeds are stones. Hailstones,
heads. Crusts of wind. Crumbs
of light. Fairweather. Hoodwinking.

Days are three-legged and prone
to wander off. Gunpowder, like sugar,
is hard-pressed to heels of hands.
Fingers bottleneck. Hearts
saloon. Like hounds
the snow surrounds.

You were expecting … what?
Storm clouds to pass
without rain. Buzzards to circle
without intent. Wind to never exceed
a breeze. On each mounting peak,
a cavalcade –

700,000 decibels of air
will barrel through by morning.
This range will shift in tiny increments
to a new location. You cannot rely
on maps.

But you're sure – where there is will
there is strategy: what they call mountains here
must be foothills and time is in the eye
of the freeloader –

Shingles peel back, twist in tendrils
of wind. The long neck of day
spools in the elbow of an eave. You leap
into its sinking belly. Light slips
behind you. Night eats up
the moon. As always.
This one begins amiss.

Reverse Forecast

At the foot of the hill we lay
ourselves plain, hoist arm hairs
to swerve as weathervanes.

Resolute, we root
our well-built hearts, certain
we can stay this side of storm –

Sleet breaks like buckshot,
howls into the hollows
of our soft-pulp trunks.

Tiny, frigid fists
sink and grip the gristle
of our tightly knotted spines.

Lightning lacerates
loose, leafing limbs,
singes every bridging branch.

Hill gives way
to waterfall, hammers us
flush with the riverbed –

Certain we can stay
this side of decorum, steadily,
we pry our backbones free,

curve our palms into paddles,
scrape cedar carcass canoes,
stroke sternly, asserting, *surely*

surely, life is but a dream.

The Way the Cookie Crumbled

Heart-slumped, bushwhacked,
taxed, adrift, sunk,
defunct, done for, null
and void, overboard,
cut loose without a paddle,
kicked out, smashed-in,
sucker-punched, ditched,
bottom-hitched, broke,
missed the boat, smoked,
drawn and quartered, deboned,
head held in the gutter,
picked clean, creamed, tossed
like a salad, left to the wolves,
throat slit, cajoled, stabbed
in the ransacked back, cut off
at the knees up to the eyeballs,
butchered, wing clipped,
stripped, bullwhipped, crushed
like a grape strung out
to dry, fed to the lions, fired
to a crisp, knuckle-
sandwiched, holding on
with nothing left
but bruise.

Notes Toward Suburbia

Think of it as music –
the wrong note will make you nervous.

This one is a low-speed, double-decker passenger train

This one is needles and hooves

This one is a humdinger
This one comes too soon

This one is the long hall

This one dips and slides

This one takes the back seat

This one is an icebreaker

This one keeps thinking of its mother

This one is more manly than the others

This one is *Australopithecus robustus*

This one says give it time

This one hangs on sisterly thoughts

This one begs for bone

This one wants a home

This one thinks, *Sabrina, Bernice*

This one plays the odds

This one is a cul-de-sac

This one is height, sudden cliff

This one is made of mist

This one is roots loosening

This one is fumbling for river

This one is an unknowable antlered mammal

This one is a bottomless O

This one stops the heart

This one comes to terms

This one is sap

This one shakes in its boots

This one is startled spruce

This one plots its next move

This one is holding back

This one is a black hole

The one you have trouble swallowing

The one struggling to be alone

This one wants to retire

This one loses its nerve

This one sells the house

This one says toughen up

This one is swinging a nine iron

This one is Florida

Before Meteorologists

With rain we gauge the split rail's give
and take, the shimmy-shake of a chair leg,
power lines that wheedle, break. We take
it to the limit, risk high points, follow bird paths,
circle just once before landing.

In the way robins seize mayflies passing
and gliders dissolve into flittering bees,
we are swollen clouds fraying, flyways faltering,
snow-struck and wind-strung. The only space
is the space collapsing space creates.

It comes down to this: final drop, a single flick
of finger lightning. At this elevation our last
comforting thought is a spontaneous generation:
a transubstantiation of horsehair to snake,
clump of mud to snail, hailstone to whooping crane.

The Proof Is in the Pudding II

Tell me, will this weight hold?

Is gravity different here?

Come on, is there no measure?

It's terrible what the ear wants

This town is a festering avocado shell

It's where some come to pool

Will anyone make it back?

Not likely

I should send postcards

You've gotten ahead of yourself

Watch the rain

It falls

Yes

III
Falsifications

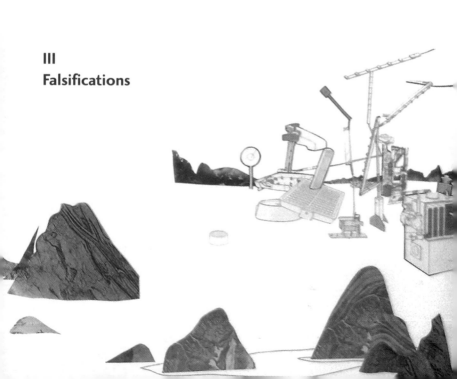

House of Cards

We wake to a carcass of cloud cover,
skeletons of lightning –

We hold one another
like the shorter ends of sticks,

as though we are the last of the baskets
for what remains of our eggs;

knowing that, apart, the night
would mistake one of us for its moon,

or when the world returns to water
each of us would be one item shy.

Nouveau Riche

At every gala extraordinaire
there's the deflated balloon
and a buffoon to boot. If only
you had bought the belle bouffant
or worn the rouge royale
then you would be chez nous-ing
with the mustachioed gent on the dance floor,
instead of leaving with your former lover,

ten years under his belt, all belly up.
Like the saying goes: you can pick
your pals, but not your beaux.
He's neither brute nor prince.
He's an ape, the perdant
who couldn't escape acne or wedgies
in the school hallway, the chump who made you
flee town, eat brie, down wine.

But this is not a setback. At breakfast
you order le bol de fruit, your espresso noir.
You have all day to shop for a très chic dress.
Tonight it's Lobster Fest! And the waiter,
Pierre, is there. In his section, you daub
Christian Dior No. 8, request their best
aperitif. You know, you know he winks
to crown you his dauphine.

Wetherspoons

You spot her wasp-waisted in a woollen wrap,
waiting for you to woo her from wineskin,
or with wild wren wrestled to the spit.
With a wily wink she sinks her teeth in,
weeds you out, well-wrought from the whacked.
In no time flat, she has you warbling,
while white-knuckled wannabes wheedle
behind your back, wince at every whisker-
close whisper you hatch. Inside whetstone mouths
they rasp words of warning: *Watch your stash!*
She's a will-o'-the-wisp! She'll lead you
widdershins! She mutters madly: *These men*
are maleficent! Make maelstrom of maps!
Mind their mines, mauling mouths, morphing masks!

Seasonal Menu

Where –
clouds let go,

whites widen,
in the crotch

of a branch,
accumulation

like sap, tapped
from pine,

snapped
from shaft,

augured
from pond,

chopped
from marrow,

chainsawed
from hock.

Where –
suet blizzards,

swallow,
wolf, drift.

Ice Fishing

Bowled over for months, the lake is stiff and ornery.
It is not in the mood. An opening the size of a cereal
bowl is augured. But this is no muskie hole, no warm
entry into the body. This is where we nip whiskey,
vie over gaff hooks, get lippy. No make-out sessions.
No snowed-in affairs. Only jigs, leaders and reels
allowed. Size and weight a slur between us; a chill.
If this temperature holds it will take thirty days
for the ice to break. Until then, anything goes.

Each human spinal column consists of thirty-three
vertebrae. Under our frigid mitted fingertips, they
are poker chips. We weigh risks, calculate odds. One
of us is all in.

No more nicey-nice. No capades. Under stolid sheets
of lake a backbone bumps. A block of snow grows
in the throat. So it goes. Just for the sake of it. Just
to save face. Not eat crow.

For anyone who has stayed up late to watch the lake

It's a porn channel
that won't tune in –

squat white homes
spreading lips,

star-spackled night
flinching,

moon and bruised canoe
bobbing.

Anchorless in a storm of limbs –
you think, *Swim.*

Field Guide to Spring

With snow it is hard to know swamp
from sturdy ground, when to trust
deer prints for depth.

Instead, listen
for water's rush, warmer weather gurgling
out winter's cached air.

Or look
to the base of willows
for water rings, wood rich with rot.

At all times
know where to find
high ground –

Swamps are predatory,
camouflage footfalls
with shifts of drifts.

If ever you mistake
the gap between trees
for path, find yourself

at the centre on a skin
of milk, consider
yourself sunk.

Artificial Reef

Tail lights like aortic valves
bore from the harbour's bottom-
feeding organ,
sputtering plankton
and diesel to the surface.

You catch red in your periphery,
a radio tower's pulse.
Hiss of water on bulbs,
the wipers' muffled rant.

Swim hard. At the bottom of this
there is a man, his mouth a clam
shucked of sound.

Übermensch

The horse breaks open, a limb sticks out, then another,
until the whole man slithers to earth. Alone
in the forest he is always in danger. And very human.
Man after man pours out. When enough are packed
shoulder to shoulder, he steps outside the portals
of the pines. Off the path.

*

There is a river digging out the spine of town,
systematizing crawling parts. Life and limbs piling
to the fringe. Winter nights may keep us crowded
precisely, but they also tease the seams.
Through every one, he slips out.

The Tin Woodman Turns Partisan

He counts our apples as he would
the dead: each one a head.

Apple strudel, apple pie,
apple crisp, apple sauce –

What we've lost will not return
to saplings, nor nourish him

for long. His axe will certainly slicken
the rest of us to saccharine, to rot.

All but one, of course. One apple
to hold above the horizon

like a sappy sunset, the aperture
of his eye. Though, he opines,

not quite round enough, not quite
as firm. This one's a wizened

son of a bitch, one
he is sure to candy,

stuff inside his growing cabinet
of atrocities.

Roadside Hideaway

Duck. Take refuge, sitting duck
or you'll be soup, or stew,
a dead duck, in any case.
And no one wants to be a smoking
duck, even if those duck tales
did become you. You ugly
duckling, you. You are more
than I can chew. My baby duck,
I'll duck you like you've never
been ducked before. I'm a duck-
hunting duck-hound. Duck down,
as in cover up, or spread
a place to put your quilty head.
I'll protect you. It'll be like water
down a duck's backside, or shooting
a duck in the bucket. A duck
test. You'll take to it like a duck
to a pond, I promise. Should we
call it a duck or a dip? A drop
in the ducky? Don't be a sour fowl.
As soon as you get your ducklings
in a row, it'll be *ducky-doodle-do*
all night through. Don't make me
go wild duck on you. I'll render you
my decoy, my rub-a-dub-dub
playmate. That's right, quack for me.
My lame mallard, I light this candle
made of fat just for you.

Rail-bent Men

Scaling chain-link with boot toes too broad
for the holes, the Dobermans' mouths below
grow into empty bowls, barbs
like army ants stinging at our wrists.

Over and down, we crawl under
the flashlight beam, the muck suckling
at our elbows and knees, our bodies
tight to the cuffs of weeds.

The freight train's smoke tugs at our sleeves,
stokes us to pick up speed. The whistle
wails a path to the tracks, where at long
last, we're at our fabled boxcar.

Inside, stowed like oats, or rogue animals
subdued by rails, we stuff our throats closed,
chew our tongues through, pray
that silos, not bullets, will halt our hearts.

With Every Departure

There is a tossed doll in high weeds.
To put out an APB is like pissing away
the wind or parking your heart
before the horse. There's just no making nothing
into a meal, or making shit that's hit the fan
whole again. So you fix

the bucket not with a doctor, Dear
Diary or Savage Love, but with a really buff
diamond or royal gala of your eye.
You know how you gotta roll
with the brie wheels downhill?
This is one of those times. Make a clean

whistle, so later when you're lying in it,
it'll be a dog and gorilla show. You'll be
Humpty Dumpty with all the king's men
to mend your fenders. Who says you can't
teach an old dog that to miss the boat
is not the same as missing the goat that fed you.

Flukes

[To begin

Metaphor #1:]

Let us eat a nourishing supper. Watch TV.
Walk until cement wears out our feet.
Sink into rubble.

Let us bumble through brambles. Smash grass.
Hew the legs of eagles as though saplings.
Rebuke wannabe lumberjacks.
Husk diamondbacks. Parade audacity.

With catfish, let's blot the moon.
Chew clouds through.
Shake hummingbirds from seaweed.
Tenderize broods.

Let's never go back. Only revise.

[Precisely two minutes pass.
A second metaphor overlays
the first.

Two more minutes
and a third begins

(exactly four minutes
into the first). And so on.

To end on

Metaphor #7:]

Let's clear out the moon,
make room for flukes. Unless
you think there's time
to systematize our ascent,
miraculously push past the slapdash.

How about we say, if our next footfalls sink
as far as sunset, we will navigate by gut,
mate like bottleflies, abandon our wineglass
torsos and shrunken corneas, put no stock
in statistics or compasses, or look to bear scat,
deer tracks or snapped branches for cues.

Call it.
Yes, I think it's correct to say,
we are out of time. Already over
our heads. In it for the long
capricious haul.

[A nine-second pause.

The interview:]

*What do you feel is the role
of lying in your work?*

An opossum can play dead
for up to six hours. In less than one second
an octopus can change colour, shape,
texture. It is also flounder, sea snake,
lionfish. It is inevitable.

What is the difference
between good and bad?

I believe we are nearly everything.

Slowly, we are being obliterated.

Is time central to this understanding?

I am not a physicist.

I can only tell you, it was by fluke
the woman was trapped in the windowless
bathroom with the deadly wasp.

I have heard this story before,
but with a scorpion.

A scorpion stuck with the wasp?

No, no. A woman and a scorpion.

Same thing.

Okay, let's not lose track.
What did you mean by 'fluke'?

Ah, now we are back
to octopuses.

Throw me a bone.

Like I said, I am
not a physician.

Tips For Remembering Who You Are

Think of a fruit, your favourite
song, gingko biloba. Recite it
every day. Use pegwords, palaces.
Macramé the constellations.
Confer with shorebirds. Call
your father. Note the fluttering
connections. Mix tapes. Take
photos. Wear layers. Polish
the cerebral corvette. Drink
milk. Digest detailed dental
records. Sport the subliminal.
Go to Harvard. Support
the hippocampus, the amygdala.
Tie a sling around it. Fish
for geneticists, neuroscientists.
Cast clairvoyants. Invest
in the Neural Impulse Actuator.
Take stock in Hitachi. Test-drive
your epoch machine. Donate
and double-bag your organs. Feed
your brain 1.9 metres. Wear a lifejacket,
helmet or hardhat. Use Oil of Olay,
formaldehyde. Exorcise. Observe
phantom limbs. Sweep
pathways clear. Keep your eyes
on past prizes. Pray
to your inner anima. Run like hell,
you're an elephant. Convince yourself.

IV
Conclusions

Nothing to Write Home

We are tents without pegs,
posts at odd angles, anchors

scraping bottom. We are thin-
limbed and ligamentless,

susceptible to the lift
of a solitary sparrow. Words

fall nebulous, night
flaps open, stars slip to the edge

of lustre. We turn black blizzard,
tender and imperceptible as a gasp

from a last wasp. Exhausted,
we avalanche

into flimsy-hearted
swans and slumping honeysuckle,

stumble into absence.

We wanted this.

We are this.

Orphans I

The cockpit of a spaceship. Unspecified time.
An expansive window faces outer space
where a mist-like entity stirs.

[Plato stands, his back to the window.]

PLATO:
I wish to speak of how
I ought to speak, and only then –

MULK RAJ ANAND:
In the smoky atmosphere,
ghosts form.

STEPHEN HAWKING:
Evidence of black holes.

HERODOTUS:
Bodies being consumed.

PLATO:
I wish to speak –

MULK RAJ ANAND:
But there is a smouldering rage!

STEPHEN HAWKING:
Light like cannonballs.

MULK RAJ ANAND:

The soundless speech of cells.

STEPHEN HAWKING:

Rather, balloons.

HERODOTUS:

Filled with pure bruise.

Orphans II

The cockpit of a spaceship. Continuous time.

PLATO:
> … of how
> I ought to speak –

MULK RAJ ANAND:
> Squeaks.

PLATO:
> I wish to speak –

MULK RAJ ANAND:
> Keep quiet.

PLATO:
> I –

[Hawking slips between the quibbling two.
Anand and Plato orbit erratically.]

STEPHEN HAWKING:
> Move away from each other.
> Maintain a constant radius.

[A minute passes in silence.]

HERODOTUS:
> Now, return to the family
> without further fuss.

STEPHEN HAWKING:
    Coalesce.

PLATO:
    I wish to –

MULK RAJ ANAND:
    You are beyond reach.

PLATO:
    How –

STEPHEN HAWKING:
    Men! We are at an end
    of time.

HERODOTUS:
    Inside our own tomb.

    [At the window the mist-like entity pulls at Plato's vision.]

PLATO:
    I wish to speak –

STEPHEN HAWKING:
    The universe must have begun –

MULK RAJ ANAND:
    Man is born, and reborn.

HERODOTUS:
    Fully formed in the womb.

PLATO:

  The desire of the whole –

STEPHEN HAWKING:

  A singularity.

PLATO:

  Love –

  [Light fades.]

Spalding

An awkward game
plays out beyond the portable.

One amateur serve
after another.

Lobs aiming to be suave
fall out of bounds.

Balls bleat. Peach fuzz
sheds across the clay court.

Strings sing, *Smash-bang the ball.*
A coach hollers, *Hold the racquet low!*

Backhands dole painstaking blows,
so much so, sneakers go squeamish.

The loudspeaker squeals, *Love, love, love …*
One discovers topspin. The same one

takes advantage –

And To Hold

Like parallel knives
the two of you

cleaving through the pinafore
of morning –

While one splits a peach
the other halves remainders

till there's nothing to split
and have. By noon

it's just the pit,
with no payoff

except to sit
on the butcher's block

intact.

Driving with Another's Lover

Spinning out, the car strips gravel, shreds rubber
to the rims, wraps metal around them
like leftovers.

Two locals discover the crash.
Rubberneckers, hubcap collectors
known least for their tact –

showing me hub after hub,
their gallery of lugs, wallets,
wedding bands in Tupperware

before finally handing me the proof I paid for:
a photograph of the aftermath, their bodies
mouths and mouths apart.

The Long Way Home

If the distance between You and Me
is the hypotenuse of right angle You-B-Me,

then the line You to Me is also a shortcut,
or a way of underscoring You-B-Me

as the long way around, and moreover,
a preposterous waste of time. But what if

that point in the future where You eventually
becomes Me is impossible to nail down

without first passing through B? This then becomes
proof that chasing the hypotenuse is the same

as tracing rainbows, and an argument for twenty-
twenty hindsight. Depressing, I know. An 'us'

stuck in the nebulous circularity of wanting again
and again to bypass B, and the 'if only' –

hence, You and Me without B is not so much
shortcut as it is deficiency.

Grey Matter

At the base of every brain sits the drain
to the heart. A siphon that strains to part
wholes from slain. Below is the jugular vein,
then a slender valve where strays, catalogued
and shelved as specimens, remind you to
tend to the rends and breaks between solid
and softer matter. Missed drifters slip by
to the muscles' upper room, where as dashed
dories they tip under the hammering
tide. Some clamour, some stride to the organ's
spongy shore, others, unmoored by amour,
drop to the pith's lower floor. And just when
you think they can sink no more, what's heard
but a dirge, its shambling bass, storied purrs.

Nervous System

In this region: lightning
unbundles too soon,

an onslaught of moon
scathes down the spine,

a sudden flurry of stars
bashes through branches.

You think,

there are other omens to show you
you are dying: the mass of birds

taking three days to pass, a shock
of meat inside the mollusc

scarcely holding it together, leaves
flipping like coins.

Outer Space Comes on as a Stranger Would in the Woods

Stars stampede through canopy toward you. Nebulas'
hands clutch your elbow too tight. Constellations
of wives descend brandishing an off-white wedding dress.
Somewhere, at an ascension unknown within you,
a long satin ribbon stirs, ripples

like milk. Hunter and hare pause, dutifully button up
their Sunday best. They've seen this too often: the chase
that becomes the ceremony, the craving for darkness
with corners, the hope that this is just a fairytale
that happens to involve dwarves and dark

matters. Yes, this whirring is only the Cuisinart,
a vacuum powering up for a good suck. Hawking
is in the living room, popping wheelies in his new
motorized chair while he postulates about cavities.
I can live like this, you think. *I can be the hired help*

as long as they own a riding snowblower and don't mind me
wearing earplugs. Each night you will help Stephen to bed,
watch back-to-back episodes of *csi Miami,* fall victim
to the Magic Bullet infomercial, dream it is a rocket
blending the space-time continuum into a delicious smoothie.

Yes, good things are spiralling toward you.

Best Foot Forward

Now that dogs can talk they rant
about non-verbal dogs chasing tail.
How so-and-so is after so-and-so
and so on. They call them mutts,
morons, keep them locked
outdoors. Smoke clove cigarillos,
sip cognac, bitch over whining strays.
They turn their muzzles up at terms
like *doggie-style*, *doggone it*, *hot dog*
and *diggity*. Cockeyed, they reminisce
over their own dog-day brawls,
dodgy racetrack and junkyard layovers.

Still, these pooches will never lose
their cool, grow lonely or bow-wow
their brains out. They'll always be dogs
of their word. In a dog-eat-dog world,
straight from the horse's mouth:
civilized dogs are top dogs.
Ask the one upstairs.

Timescale Chauvinism

> *Music is the pleasure the human mind experiences from counting without being aware that it is counting.*
> – Gottfried Leibniz

I

At what point will I realize
my mind is slipping?

*When you admit
you are your mind.*

You've changed.

*And your intellect takes you to the stink
of volcanoes.*

Solipsist.

*How can you be so sensitive?
You're barely sentient.*

It's a difficult descent.

[Like locusts
the violinists twitch.]

II

When we are an ear bone's throw from balance
what sea saws our inner labyrinth? What strays

from the tympanic path? Solid objects
turn soluble. Cerebellums unlatch.

Sound becomes space. Here today,
ghost limbs tomorrow, dissipating

snow. Whether it is heat
or silence that makes the proximate birds

fall slack inside us, we are convinced
there is a connection to lack.

[A piano strides into technical
explorations, without story,

where tempo fails.]

III

Someone once said, *Atoms are all colourless;*
of whatever hue you perceive the bodies, do not be duped.

Beyond our reach, hydro lines boast achromatic
crowsong. Trees slough free their perjuring leaves.

These are the stiff conceits we outwardly scoff at,
but unwittingly grasp. To step back

will not assist us in being more than molecular
plankton fodder. We are invariant with delusions

of other. No matter how we spin it.

[The choir flattens under
the conductor's deadpan palm.]

Self-Destruction Manual: Bridge Jumper

Empty your pockets, there's a river
rushing toward you from below. Throw
paper items first. Let birds gather
torn notes, make a nest out of knowing
you couldn't make it. Toss your watch.
Time it well. A walloped fisherman
could make your last moments woeful.
Now, rid yourself of coins, cigarettes, gum.
Then, move on to weightier items – this
buys you time to lose the shoes. Be sure
to save the heaviest possession for
the final fling – in case you change your mind.
This will burst the water's tension wide,
so your body can slip, unremarkably, in.

Determinism vs. Neuroplasticity

What if it's the oddballs who are stacked against you,
ready to skew every system you use? So that the loons

you call drifters are, and always have been, crazies.
And snow slipping from a roof is a limp

shoe-size family soaring toward you – a jewellery box
of jays, a change purse of field mice. Makes birds

or rodents in hand better than those in ambush.
Keeps skies clear. Leaves no room for style

of clock you'll buy, or that goslings adopt any moving
object as mother. But what if all these thoughts change brain

configurations; or what's more, if the chunk the brain thinks
it's thinking with is changing too? Does this not make sense –

a series of loose ends? Prove the mind will make nightmares
out of anything? We've all watched moths

throwing themselves against headlights, dogs barking
into wallpapered rooms, cashiers struggling to make

eye contact. There's just no telling *which* end is loosest.

Rodeo Romance

She pulls on her chaps, cowgirl hat,
walks past congregated grass
to the mall.

Champing at the bit,
her well-oiled bull
fits for the clink of a coin –

every day they make their getaway,
ride off into the sun display,
some unhappy heifer after.

Ambitious Birds

As certainly as rain runs down a cheek,
runways run below the airplane window,
molecules part, relocate, reform.

A yellow warbler buries parasitic broods
under an escalating tower of fresh nests.
She forsakes her own unborn

smothered underneath. Lays
new eggs. For some, abandonment
brings glossy T-birds, the penthouse suite.

It is lunacy to look down. It is doing
what comes instinctively that propels us upward.
There are birds, then there are better birds.

Notes

The opening quote is from Terry Pratchett's novel *Lords and Ladies* (HarperTorch, 1996).

The lines in the third stanza of 'Solubles', referencing the theory of memory and water are derived from Dr. Jacques Benveniste's article 'Understanding Digital Biology' (1998).

The epigraph for 'Sound Check' was found at Wikipedia's page on 'Literal Translation,' paraphrased from John Hutchins' article '"The whisky was invisible," or Persistent myths of MT,' found in *MT News International* 11 (June 1995). The poem was inspired by the online resource for Respiratory Assessment: http://www.scribd.com/doc/9905585/Respiratory-Assessment-Skills.

The first stanza of 'Law of Averages' is borrowed from Patrick Suskind's novel *Perfume: The Story of a Murderer* (Alfred A. Knopf, 1986).

The epigraph for 'Almanac' is a line from Ann-Marie MacDonald's *The Way the Crow Flies* (Alfred A. Knopf, 2003).

'Übermensch' began as found lines from the following texts: *The Stone Age Present: How Evolution Has Shaped Modern Life-From Sex, Violence, and Language to Emotions, Morals, and Communities* by William F. Allman (Simon & Schuster, 1994); *Achilles: A Novel* by Elizabeth Cook (Picador, 2003); *The Lives of a Cell* by Lewis Thomas (Bantam, 1984); *The Bloody Chamber: And Other Stories* by Angela Carter (Penguin, 1987).

The first response of the interview appearing in 'Flukes' contains animal facts found at Wikipedia's page on the television documentary *The Most Extreme*.

'Orphans I' and 'Orphans II' are 99.9 percent comprised of found lines from the following texts: 'Untouchable,' *Selected Short Stories of Mulk Raj Anand*, edited by M. K. Naik (Arnold-Heinemann, 1977); *A Brief of History of Time* by Stephen Hawking (Bantam, 1998); *The Histories* by Herodotus, ed. John M. Marincola, trans. Aubrey De Selincourt (Penguin Books, 1996); and *Symposium* by Plato, translated by Alexander Nehamas and Paul Woodruff (Hackett Pub Co, 1989).

The epigraph in 'Timescale Chauvinism' is borrowed from *Wonders of Numbers: Adventures in Mathematics, Mind, and Meaning* by Clifford A. Pickover (Oxford University Press, 2002). The italicized lines in Part III are a paraphrase of the same concept found in Galileo Galilei's *The Assayer* (1616).

Acknowledgements

Some of these poems, in one incarnation or another, were published in literary journals: *The Fiddlehead, Prism international, Prairie Fire*; and in anthologies: *I.V. Lounge Nights, Fevered Spring Almost Instant Anthology, The Hoodoo You Do So Well* and *This Grace*. Thanks to the editors and publishers.

Thank you to Coach House Books and *Arc* magazine in conjunction with the Ontario Arts Council's Writer's Reserve Program, as well as the Canada Council for the Arts and the Conseil des arts et des lettres du Québec for their financial support.

Thank you also to the Banff Centre for the Arts, Writing Studio 2007 and 2011 for the time, space and inspiration to write – the king-size bed was also marvellous! My heartfelt appreciation goes out to Jan Zwicky, Don McKay, John Barton, Barry Dempster, Carolyn Forché and Elizabeth Philips for their masterful eyes and minds.

An enormous thank you to Alana Wilcox, Evan Munday and Leigh Nash of Coach House Books for the many hours they dedicated to making my first book and publishing experience wonderful. And Kevin Connolly, what can I say, your brilliance as an editor is awe-inspiring.

Above all, my deepest gratitude to Jeramy Dodds, Joshua Trotter, Gabe Foreman, Linda Besner and Daniel Renton for their devotion. If it weren't for them, this book would have had a crowd of awkward moments. Daniel, you've been a rock. To Zach Gaviller, Aliya Dalfen, Amy Chartrand, Sara Fleury and Jenny Gleeson, who have also seen to me and/or my work over the years. To Joe, Rebecca, Caleb, Eli, Anita, Saleema, Jerry, Charmaine, Danielle, Katia, Greg, the other Zach, Sigrun, Rylan, A. J., Jamie, Bryce, Lisa, Gavin, Sam, Chrissy, Carrie, Jen, Jennie, Sandy, Sarah, Lindsay (a.k.a. Bird) and Gregg for their friendship. To Guanajuato, Mexico, for the ardour. And to my family, for their endless support.

This book is dedicated to the memory of my brother Greg and nephew David, for whom sadly there are no words. You are deeply missed.

About the Author

Leigh Kotsilidis grew up in Niagara Falls, Ontario. In 2009 and 2010 she was selected as a finalist for the CBC Literary Awards. She is also co-founder of littlefishcartpress. She currently lives in Montreal.

Typeset in Charlotte and Charlotte Sans
Printed and bound at the Coach House on bpNichol Lane, 2011

Edited by Kevin Connolly
Designed by Alana Wilcox
Cover art and details throughout book: Holli Schorno, *Signal Hill*,
    2008, Book Cuttings on Paper. Courtesy of the Artist and the
    International Collage Center Collection

Coach House Books
80 bpNichol Lane
Toronto ON M5S 3J4

416 979 2217
800 367 6360

mail@chbooks.com
www.chbooks.com